Original title:

Watering Wednesday

Copyright © 2025 Creative Arts Management OÜ

All rights reserved.

Author: Liam Sterling
ISBN HARDBACK: 978-1-80581-722-2
ISBN PAPERBACK: 978-1-80581-249-4
ISBN EBOOK: 978-1-80581-722-2

Glimmers of Green

In the garden, plants do dance,
With spouts and hoses, not by chance.
A sprinkle here, a splash on toes,
Who knew plants had such funny woes?

Gnomes in rows, they laugh and cheer,
As I trip over roots, oh dear!
The daisies giggle, can't you see?
They love the chaos, oh so free!

Bubble baths for leafy friends,
Not all care for their leafy bends.
A watering can, my playful foe,
It spills and splutters, oh what a show!

Sunshine smiles on every leaf,
While I wrestle with my grief.
But here comes rain to save the day,
Now my garden leads the play!

Raindrop Reverie

A droplet danced upon my head,
It whispered secrets, rainbows spread.
My plants wore hats of shiny dew,
They laughed at how I slipped and flew.

The cat joined in, a soggy sight,
He twirled, he leaped, oh what a fright!
The garden gnome, with grin so wide,
Enjoyed the splash, no need to hide.

Midweek Mist

A fog rolled in, all thick and gray,
My coffee asked me, 'Is it May?'
I tripped on puddles, shoes afloat,
A rubber duck became my boat.

The sun peeked out, a cheeky glare,
It winked, like it just didn't care.
With every spray, the flowers cheered,
'Leave it to us, we're not afraid!'

Hues of Hydration

With watering cans, we made a mess,
The dog got drenched, what a distress!
In colors bright, the blooms they danced,
While squirrels stopped by, completely pranced.

And then my friend, with hose in hand,
Gave every plant a funny stand.
A rainbow formed, the birds in line,
'Can we get a sip?' they asked, just fine!

Cultivating Calm

The garden gloves were much too thick,
I missed the pot, it made me sick.
With mud on hands and dirt on nose,
I chuckled loud, it's how it goes!

So let it rain, let laughter flow,
With every splash, I'll let you know.
In plants we trust, with jokes and fun,
Midweek mayhem, we've just begun!

Nurtured by Raindrops

The plants are dancing, feeling grand,
A droplet party, oh so planned.
They sip and giggle, such a sight,
While we all dash from left to right.

Umbrellas flip, like fish in flight,
A soggy sock takes off with fright.
The garden glee, a splashy play,
As flowers laugh the clouds away.

The Gentle Thirst

The daisies whisper, 'Oh, we need!'
A sweet refreshment, yes indeed.
They stretch and yawn, all green and bright,
While crickets play a tune tonight.

A raindrop bounces on my nose,
I giggle at the splash that goes.
The breeze joins in, all full of cheer,
As thirsty blooms bring joy, oh dear!

Midweek Rains

Halfway through the week we pause,
To cheer on each sprout with applause.
The garden hose takes the stage,
As plants break out in a wild rage.

The worms join in, a muddy fest,
With each sunbeam, they twirl their best.
So here we are, what a fun show,
With every drop, the laughter grows.

Garden's Embrace

The water dribbles, splashes wide,
A funny dance, we can't abide.
Each petal shakes, a giggly tune,
As bumblebees buzz 'neath the moon.

The misty breeze, it tickles my cheek,
As colorful petals start to sneak.
We pop some popcorn, plant a seed,
Midweek fun, it's all we need!

Petals and Potential

Sprinkling the garden with joy and glee,
Watch the daisies dance, oh what a spree!
Lettuce whispers secrets as it grows tall,
While carrots plot mischief, oh my, not at all!

The tears of the soil, they giggle and gleam,
As seeds throw a party, it's more than a dream!
Butterflies flap their wings in delight,
While worms dance like crazy, what a silly sight!

Nature's Alchemy

In the garden of mayhem where veggies conspire,
Tomatoes dressed up, set the world on fire!
Radishes wear hats, so witty and bright,
As herbs crack jokes under the pale moonlight.

The rain clouds come rolling, in habits so bold,
They splash on the flowers, not caring, just cold!
Lettuce laughs loudly, it's a leafy affair,
While peas plan a prank, oh, do they dare?

Echoes of Ebb

Puddles reflect giggles from hydrating skies,
Jumping in raindrops, what a great surprise!
Squirrels try sailing on waves made of dew,
While frogs play the banjo, what a marvelous crew!

The rivers hum tunes, quite chatty today,
Fish wear tiny hats, they won't float away!
With splashes and laughter, all creatures partake,
In this watery dance, there's no time to shake!

Sprinkling Sunshine

Showering the flowers with mirth in the sun,
Bees buzzing loudly, oh, aren't they just fun?
Cacti wear sunglasses, they're cool as can be,
While sunflowers flex, as tall as a tree!

The garden is grinning with all of its cheer,
And gnomes stilt walk, tiptoeing near!
Rains share their jokes, with bubbles and flair,
In this playful ballet, there's joy everywhere!

Gentle Showers

Raindrops tap dance on the ground,
Plants start a giggle, oh so sound.
Umbrellas flip like they're in a race,
As puddles form a splashing place.

Garden gnomes join in the fun,
Juggling raindrops just for a run.
Frogs croak jokes, the worms all cheer,
This wet parade is the highlight here!

Life's Liquid Embrace

The hose is like a magic wand,
Sprinkling smiles across the land.
With every squirt, a giggle flies,
As friends try dodging, oh what a prize!

The neighbors peek through windows wide,
Wondering where all the giggles hide.
Chasing each other, they run with zest,
An unexpected midday fest!

Dewy Dreams

Morning mists, oh what a sight,
Dewdrops sparkle, it feels just right.
Ants have parties on blades of green,
While sunbeams dance, a joyful scene.

Grass tickles toes, laughter rings clear,
It's a paradise, joy is near.
With every sip, the flowers grin,
In this refreshing, funny spin!

Whispering Brooks

Brooks babble tales, a gurgling spree,
Sharing secrets with a leaf or three.
Fish jump up with a comical splash,
Creating quite the aquatic bash!

With stones that giggle and currents that play,
Nature's joke book is on display.
While rubber ducks float with great flair,
Rich with laughter in the cool, crisp air!

When Clouds Weep

When clouds burst out in laughter,
The garden splashes with cheer.
Worms wear tiny rain boots,
Dancing round without fear.

Puddles become little lakes,
Where frogs host a swim race.
They leap with glee in the air,
Hoping to win first place.

Thunder cracks like a joke,
As flowers shake in delight.
They rattle their petals down,
Letting loose in the light.

With raindrops as fizzy drinks,
The plants toss back their heads.
Each drop is a tickle giggle,
While soaking their leafy beds.

Bright Blossoms Await

The garden wakes up with a yawn,
Colorful blooms stretch and sway.
They tickle the sun with their petals,
In a cheeky flower ballet.

Bees buzz in for a giggle,
With their tiny polka dot suits.
They mischief about the tulips,
Stealing nectar like fruits.

Sunflowers face the bright sky,
With shades of yellow so bold.
They wink at the passing clouds,
Wearing hats made of gold.

As daisies laugh in the breeze,
They whisper secrets so sweet.
A snicker behind their leaves,
'Til the next neighbor they greet.

Constellations of Color

Underneath a glittering sky,
Flowers bloom as though stars.
They twinkle a rainbow of dreams,
With petals like candy bars.

Tulips play hide and seek,
In a field that's dressed in dye.
While daisies blow silly kisses,
To butterflies passing by.

The sun casts a golden glow,
Spreading cheer over the land.
As colors frolic and tumble,
In a whimsical flower band.

Forget all the busy tasks,
Let's celebrate the bright show.
For in this patch of wonder,
We'll let our laughter flow.

The Savor of Spring

Spring arrives in a goofy hat,
Leading a parade of fun.
With choirs of chirping crickets,
Singing tunes on the run.

Each seed sows a silly story,
As it sprouts with a grin.
A carrot winks from the dirt,
And says, 'Let the snacking begin!'

Beets blush deep shades of red,
As they giggle and shake.
While onions burst into tears,
From the laughter they make.

So grab a bowl of fresh veggies,
And munch with joy, don't delay.
In the garden of giggles,
Every bite's a bright play!

An Oasis in Time

In a garden, spades dance and twirl,
Dirt flies high, what a messy swirl!
The flowers giggle, the weeds take flight,
As gloves are lost in a grand delight.

A hose parade winds through the mud,
Little toads cheer, 'Oh what a dud!'
With every splash, a new plan unfolds,
While sunburned noses, their stories told.

As petals sip from cups thrown wide,
The sunbeams join in, side by side.
But wait! What's that? A squirrel's on the run,
Making off with the radish, thinking it's fun!

When can we plant? Well, that's the jest,
For every gardener knows, it's just guessing the rest.
With seeds in hand and helmeted heads,
We water our dreams where laughter spreads.

Nature's Respite

In the garden, all's in bloom,
A sandwich shared with the local loom.
Bees buzz softly, they know the tune,
While ants throw a party beneath the moon.

Rabbits hop in their Sunday best,
While flowers tease them — it's all a jest!
'Hey there, buddy, your fur's a mess!'
But the rabbit winks, 'I'm just here to impress!'

Droplets drizzle from overhead,
A curious bird finds a cozy bed.
Each squirt from the hose, quite the show,
Gives the garden a splash, ready to grow.

But oh! What's that? A gopher alarms,
As he digs deep, seeking out charms.
Yet laughter abounds, for nature's a prank,
In this quirky greenhouse, we're all quite tanked!

The Gift of Growth

With trowel and cheer, we head outside,
Planting dreams where the worms abide.
Tomatoes wear hats, they look so grand,
While pumpkins plot world domination, unplanned.

A cowbell rings, can you hear it chime?
That's the lettuce, saying it's lunchtime.
But carrots just grin, hiding their roots,
While cauliflowers dream of disco suits.

The skies above bring a gentle tease,
As rain clouds waggle, 'What's the freeze?'
But droplets giggle, as they do their spin,
Dancing on daisies like they're at a win.

Each sprout and seed has secrets to share,
As daisies dare the dandelions to pair.
So come one, come all, let's grow with flair,
In this garden of laughter, joy fills the air!

Sowing Under Skies

In the field, we gather, a motley crew,
With hats askew and mud on our shoe.
The sun peeks out with a wink and a grin,
While squirrels debate where the fun should begin.

A hose lies coiled, in the grass it hides,
Waiting for chaos, oh how it bides!
With every squeeze, a rainbow unfurls,
As we get sprayed, and laughter swirls.

Beans take the lead, growing faster than light,
While cabbages conspire to stay out of sight.
The potatoes giggle, all snug in the ground,
Making plans for a pop-up, oh what a sound!

With dirt on our hands and joy in our hearts,
We dance with the daisies, the fun never departs.
In gardens of laughter, we sow our schemes,
For under these blue skies, life's sweeter than dreams!

Midweek Nourishment

On this day, the plants all cheer,
They shout for joy, oh, loud and clear.
With dropper in hand, I do my dance,
A soggy tango, their happy prance.

The cat laughs hard, she sloshes by,
With every step, she gives a sigh.
Wet socks abound, it's quite the show,
My green pals giggle as I slip and go!

Can we call this therapy? I say,
As I splash and smile the morning away.
For every droplet brings them glee,
And leaves me drench'd, oh joy for me!

So don't forget, when midweek's here,
Bring out your hose, it's time for cheer.
A spritz of fun for all to share,
Just mind the puddles, and avoid despair!

Floral Fountains

There's a fountain in my garden fair,
With blooms that giggle, scents fill the air.
I whip out my hose, it's time to play,
But watch your step, or you'll sway!

These flowers know just how to tease,
They shake their petals in the breeze.
I spray them gently, they bounce with glee,
"More, more!" they cry, "Oh can't you see?"

The neighbor's dog starts to bark and leap,
Wondering why my plants can't sleep.
With soil on my hands and a grin on my face,
This watering fun feels like a race!

As the sun dips low, I wave goodbye,
Tomorrow, dear flowers, we'll reach for the sky.
With laughter and joy, let's start anew,
For watering's wild, and it's just us two!

The Gift of Rain

Oh, rain, dear friend, you make me laugh,
Soaking my shoes in your bubbly bath.
With clouds above, the sky looks gray,
Yet laughter blooms on this drippy day.

I grab my tin can, full of glee,
Sending droplets to the plants with a spree.
They giggle back, in shades of bright,
"More of this fun, keep it in sight!"

The neighbors cringe as I frolic around,
Unfazed by puddles that leap from the ground.
With rain as my partner, we dance along,
This sweet little wet day just can't be wrong!

So let it pour, let's get a bit silly,
For every drop makes the flowers quite frilly.
With mud on my face and joy in my heart,
The gift of this rain? A wonderful art!

Thirsting for Growth

My plants are thirsty, they need a sip,
They wiggle and jiggle, they start to grip.
With watering can in hand, I embark,
On a drippy quest in the sunny park.

The garden beds beckon, "Oh fill us up!"
And I start pouring with a giggle and hup!
But who knew that hose could twist and twirl,
Creating puddles, making me whirl!

While daisies dance and roses bounce,
I send water flying, I can't seem to pounce!
So here I stand, a jester in green,
With a fool on each plant, oh, what a scene!

So here's to growth, and joy anew,
As I drench my garden, it's all true blue.
Just remember folks, to laugh and play,
On this day of fun, isn't that the way?

Sound of the Falling

In the garden, rain drops prance,
Each petal's dance is quite a chance.
Worms slide by, in style they boast,
Sipping tea, they play host.

Leaves whisper secrets, all around,
While puddles form a splashy sound.
Dancing raindrops make a show,
Like a shower, but with a flow.

Crickets hop, they find it grand,
As droplets tickle the thirsty land.
It's a party for the plants to thrive,
Throwing a bash, feeling alive!

With every drop, a giggle or two,
The trees sway along, it's all brand new.
Let's celebrate with muddy shoes,
Nature's whimsy, how can we lose?

Harvesting Harmony

In the fields, a merry sight,
Veggies giggle, oh what a fright!
Tomatoes argue, who's the best,
While lettuce dreams of a fancy vest.

Carrots join in, waving bright,
Telling stories of growing might.
The sun plays tag behind the clouds,
While watermelons sing out loud.

Potatoes joke with a wink and grin,
As ants march by, they nod and spin.
When rain arrives, it's pure delight,
A splash of joy, a funny sight!

Together they sway, in harmony found,
With laughter echoing all around.
In this patch, a perfect blend,
Each planted joke, a new best friend!

The Essence of Renewal

A sponge on the counter, dreams so grand,
Wishes for raindrops, oh isn't it planned?
Spilling secrets on every dish,
A sudsy dance, bubbles flash and swish!

Sprouts in kitchen pots, growing fine,
Imagining waltzes, oh how they shine!
With spritzes of mist and a tickle of foam,
They plot their escape, a plant-based roam.

The sink's overflowing, a splashy surprise,
While forks and spoons share giggly cries.
Glorious chaos, a potpourri spree,
In every drop, chuckles flow free!

So lift up your cup; let's toast the rain,
For laughter in drops is never in vain.
Every sprinkle's a chance to renew,
Beneath the sun's smile, a funny view!

Liquid Lullabies

A sip of soda sings to the glass,
Bubbles giggle as they shimmer and pass.
The ice cubes join in a chilly dance,
While straws tell stories of romance.

Splashing lemonade in bright sunny rays,
Citrus calypso brightens our days.
Cups spill secrets, it's all quite fun,
Cooling off antics while we bask in the sun.

But watch out for the splash, oh what a sight,
As kids chase droplets, their laughter takes flight.
Water balloons fly, like laughter in the air,
A fun-filled garden without a care.

So sip and swallow these liquid tunes,
As summer whispers with giggling moons.
Raise your glass high, let the fun reside,
In every drop, let laughter coincide!

Raindrops and Renewal

Splish splash, here they come,
Little drops in a jolly drum.
Puddle leaps and giggly squeals,
Muddy shoes reveal our feels.

Raincoats on, we take the stage,
Twirl like dancers, earn our wage.
Clouds above, they wink and smile,
Join us for a rain-soaked while!

Nature's shower, we embrace,
Drippy noses, splashy grace.
Echoes of our laughter soar,
Rainy days, we ask for more.

Raindrops fall with silly flair,
Chasing rainbows everywhere.
When it pours, let joy ignite,
Raindrops keep our spirits bright!

Pastoral Puddles

In fields of grass, the puddles pride,
Hopping through, let's take a ride!
Each splash tells a joke so fine,
Nature's laughter, yours and mine.

Little ducks all wiggle-waddle,
Joining in this joyful puddle.
Farmer Joe with his big old hat,
Slips and slides, oh, imagine that!

Pastoral scenes in messy play,
Swishing boots, hip-hip-hooray!
In mud pies, we shape our dreams,
Where laughter flows in bubbling streams.

Here's to frogs and jolly fun,
Bouncing in the midday sun.
Petals dance, the world twirls round,
In pastoral puddles, joy is found!

Verdant Ventures

In gardens bright, we plot our course,
With watering cans, a jolly force.
Sprays of color, here and there,
Petals giggle, scents declare!

Bees and bugs join in the fun,
Buzz and crawl, oh what a run!
Dirt on faces, grins so wide,
Nature's playground, our joyride.

Dancing weeds and sneaky snails,
Sharing secrets, funny tales.
With every plant, a story grows,
In verdant ventures, laughter flows.

So grab a trowel, let's explore,
With playful hearts, we'll want more.
In the green, we'll dream and play,
With nature's jokes, come join the fray!

Tending to Tomorrow

With tiny seeds, we plant our hopes,
In mounds of soil, laughter ropes.
Sprouts emerge with tiny grins,
In garden plots, adventure begins.

Tickled leaves and sun-soaked rays,
Gardening antics fill our days.
Birds above sing silly tunes,
While we're mud-streaked like raccoons.

A hose fight breaks out, what a scene!
Water splashes, we're so keen!
Tomorrow's blooms are giggles spry,
In our green kingdom, watch us fly.

Tending dreams that sprout and sway,
Nurtured by our carefree play.
Laughs and love, in earthy plots,
Tomorrow's joy, we'll tie our knots!

Liquid Lullabies

In the garden, plants do sway,
Hoping for rain, oh what a play!
But here comes a hose, I'm the star,
Splashing everywhere, like a silly czar!

Oh look at the daisies, they jump and dance,
They really think they've got a chance!
As I shower them with giddy might,
They grin and giggle, what a silly sight!

Puddles all around, a muddy delight,
Frogs leap in joy, it's quite a sight!
I slip and slide, oh what a spree,
The plants are laughing, so wild and free!

In my fun-filled garden, the sun does beam,
With each little splash, we're living the dream!
So here's to the laughter, the joy we cheer,
Liquid lullabies to all who draw near!

Sowing Seeds of Hope

I dropped some seeds, oh what a mess,
In little rows, I tried my best!
But the squirrels came for a jabbering feast,
Now they're the rulers, to say the least!

The sun shines bright, the soil is loose,
My garden cries, it wants a truce!
So here I come, with my trusty can,
Hoping to save this silly plan!

The flowers nod, while grass plays cheer,
Complaints of drought, oh never fear!
I sprinkle joy, a wiggly hose,
And watch as nature has its pose!

From tiny sprouts to blooms so bold,
Each splash of love, a tale to be told!
We're sowing laughter, with soil and sun,
In this whimsical garden, we have such fun!

Cascading Care

The watering can has taken flight,
I chase it down, what a silly sight!
It spills and drips, a waterfall show,
Every plant giggles, as if in the know!

With my trusty hat, I stomp around,
Each step I take, a slushy sound!
The daisies peek, with petals so bright,
They're taking bets on my next big plight!

Oh, the sun plays tricks, it's really a tease,
Shining on me, as I get on my knees!
"More, more!" the veggies chant with glee,
While I dance like a fish, oh look at me!

Each droplet cascades with the utmost care,
As laughter rings out in the warm, sweet air!
Together we grow, in this jovial dance,
Cascading care, in nature's romance!

Splashes of Serenity

In the quiet morn, with a can in hand,
I wander about through my dreamy land!
But oh, what's this? A kitten appears,
And knocks over the can, oh dear, oh dear!

With a splash and a giggle, it's all a game,
The plants join in, oh what a fame!
As I mop up the soil, the flowers cheer,
We're all soaked, but have not a fear!

Bubble, bubble, and a wiggle with joy,
This garden is playful, no need to be coy!
As rain drops shimmer, with soft little bursts,
We dance in puddles, quenching our thirsts!

So here's to the fun, in our little nook,
With splashes of serenity, nature's own book!
A splash of laughter, a drop of cheer,
In this funny garden, we hold it dear!

A Dance of Dew

Droplets twirl on blades of grass,
A tiny ballroom, oh what sass!
Frogs leap in a grand ballet,
While bugs hit the floor to sway.

Sunshine's spotlight shines so bright,
As ants join in the joyous flight.
A wobbly worm with two left feet,
Oh, how the critters dance and meet!

Clouds above hum a gentle tune,
While daisies sway—what a cartoon!
With every splash, a giggle grows,
In this garden where laughter flows.

So take a seat and watch the show,
As nature's cast steals the glow.
A raucous romp, no need to fuss,
Join the jive, come dance with us!

Earth's Tender Kiss

A gentle mist hugs the soft ground,
A cheeky breeze dances all around.
Puddles giggle, quite pleased to be,
The splashes of joy, oh can't you see?

Raindrops try to tap at leaves,
But every leaf just giggles and grieves.
The flowers bloom, all laughs and cheer,
Earth's warm embrace, let's all draw near!

Grasshoppers claim they are the stars,
Leaping high, forgetting their cars.
"Skip the ride!" they chirp with glee,
"Just hop along, come jump with me!"

The sunlight beams, a clownish grin,
Chasing clouds with a playful spin.
Each drop a kiss, so sweet, divine,
In this silly scene, all love aligns!

The Quenching Hour

Oh what a time, it's quite the spree,
The sun shines down, a funny decree.
Water pots wobble on the ledge,
As plants whisper, "Please, on this edge!"

A curious squirrel gives it a nudge,
And spills water, oh what a fudge!
"Oops, my fault!" he shouts with glee,
"Let's all get wet, you and me!"

The garden crew starts a splash fight,
While mischief dances into the night.
Where petals flutter like they're in a race,
To claim the title of the wettest place!

So grab a hose, it's time for play,
Don't be shy, come join the fray!
In nature's pool of joy and fun,
We'll laugh and drench till day is done!

Renewal's Whisper

When morning breaks, the giggles start,
A shimmer spreads, it steals the heart.
Leaves chat softly with the breeze,
Chattering secrets amongst the trees.

A playful drop clings to a stalk,
"Come on, plants, let's go for a walk!"
They skip in rhythm, oh what a sight,
With petals giggling, all pure delight.

The frogs gather 'round to lend a voice,
A croaky choir, they've made their choice.
Willow trees sway, their branches cheer,
Jumping jigs, "It's that time of year!"

So laugh along with the morning dew,
Let nature's smiles channel through you.
In each little droplet, find joy anew,
As the world spins round with a colorful hue!

Morning Dew's Delight

Early sun beams down bright,
Dewdrops dance, oh what a sight!
Leaves glisten like jewels on a spree,
Plants giggle, 'Look at me!'

A squirrel sneezes, oh what a fuss,
Dew drops fly—did he make a fuss?
Frogs croak tunes in the playful mist,
Nature's antics can't be missed!

Ants parade in a dewy quest,
Hopping joyfully, like they're blessed.
Each sip of water makes them prance,
What a funny morning dance!

So grab your cups, don't be shy,
Join the plants in their silly high!
A sip of morning, laughter anew,
In this dew, a funny brew!

Harvesting Harmony

Worms wriggle with such charm,
A garden party, no cause for alarm.
Tomatoes blush from sun's embrace,
While zucchinis wear a smiling face.

Radishes spin tales underground,
Sharing secrets, profound and sound.
They laugh as carrots tickle their toes,
A funny scene where joy just flows.

Cucumbers dance, all sprightly and bright,
Salsa dreams in the shimmering light.
Bees take breaks; they hum and sway,
Harvesting giggles along the way.

As veggies mingle, they shout, "Hooray!"
What a fun, bumpy harvest day.
So gather round, let laughter ring,
In this garden, joy is the thing!

The Ripple Effect

A drop splashed down with a wink,
Creating ripples, they start to think.
Frogs leap in, creating a show,
Making waves, don't you know?

Fish swim by with a silly grin,
"Join the splash! Where to begin?"
Turtles chuckle as they float,
In this pond, joy's the antidote!

Clouds above say, "Here, hold this!"
As rain drops down, it's hard to miss.
The whole pond giggles, what a fest,
In the fun of droplets, they're all blessed.

So when you see a puddle form,
Jump right in—get ready for warm!
Experience ripples with pure delight,
Let foolish joy take flight tonight!

Nourishing Nature's Canvas

In a garden of colors so bright,
Paintbrushes dance with morning light.
Flowers giggle, spreading their hue,
They whisper, "Look at our funny crew!"

Bees buzz by with a cheeky grin,
Mixing colors, a floral spin.
Petals blush at the cheeky jest,
Nature's canvas, simply the best!

A painter frog hops, with style so bold,
Mixing up greens, reds, or gold.
Each stroke a ripple, with laughter divine,
Where each drop of rain meets sunshine.

Canvas blooms with laughter and cheer,
A masterpiece grows, year after year.
So join the fun and make your mark,
In this silly garden, a splash, a spark!

Soaked in Serenity

I danced with a hose, what a sight,
Splashing my shoes, oh, what a delight!
The garden gnome chuckled, a grin on his face,
As I twirled and twisted in this watery race.

The cat eyed me suspiciously, quite disturbed,
While the flowers laughed loudly, feeling superb.
"Just a little more," I said with a grin,
As I soaked my socks, I knew I would win!

The birdbath overflowed, like a tiny fountain,
While I tried not to slip, scaling the mountain.
A butterfly landed, donning a crown,
In my puddle party, I'm the king of the town!

But now I'm all drenched—what a grand fuss,
Next time I'll wear swim trunks—just me and the bus!
In this soggy ballet, I've found my true cheer,
In the realm of the wet, let's all raise a beer!

Sprouts of Hope

With a sprinkle and splash, I care for my kin,
In the garden of joy, where the laughter begins.
Worms wiggle and giggle, they dance in delight,
While I drench the daisies, oh, what a sight!

The neighbor peeks over, with a look of concern,
"Why dance with the daisies?" Oh, how I learn!
"It's a sprinkle session, it's all in good fun,"
But the peonies blushed, they're sneaking a run.

The sun took a snooze, hiding behind a cloud,
I waved to the raindrops, feeling quite proud.
As the garden exploded in shades of bright glee,
Even my old boots were laughing with me!

The veggies chimed in, their leaves fluttered wide,
"Give us the juice, we've got nothing to hide!"
So I doused them in joy, what a leafy parade,
Amongst all this chaos, I'm happy I stayed!

Drizzle of Dreams

A drop on my nose sparked a curious thought,
Am I a flower? Or just getting caught?
As I pranced and splashed, I felt quite alive,
In my whimsical world, with my plant pals, I thrive.

The carrots cheered loudly, oh what a sound,
They wiggled and giggled, turning round and round.
The lettuce threw parties, with greens in the air,
In this garden soirée, I felt happy and rare!

But whoops! There's a puddle, now I'm knee-deep,
The rubarb did cackle as I took a leap.
"Join us!" they whispered, with a wave of a leaf,
In this merry mishap, I tossed all my grief.

With laughter as sweet as the raindrop's embrace,
We danced together, it was truly a race.
Under skies painted dreams, I found my own tune,
As we splashed through the night, beneath the bright moon!

Hallowed Hydration

In the garden's embrace, with a bucket in hand,
I summon the skies, let's make a wetland!
A serenade of soakers, I conduct the fun,
With daisies and dandelions, we've only begun!

The clouds start to giggle, I swear I can hear,
As I water the weeds with a grin ear to ear.
The veggies all chuckle, the herbs shake with zest,
In this grand comedy, we're all on a quest!

Oh, the basil's so sassy, it turns up its nose,
While the tomatoes blush red—what a plot twist, who knows?
I'm the captain of chaos, in this wet escapade,
As the raindrops applaud my plant-inspired parade!

So if you're feeling low, grab a hose by the end,
And join in the laughter, my sweetest of friends.
In this garden of humor, we'll splash and we'll cheer,
As we cherish the drizzles, year after year!

Beneath the Cloud's Caress

Beneath the clouds, we dance and sway,
A choreographed splash on a sunny day.
Umbrellas flip, oh what a sight,
As raindrops giggle, a joyful delight.

Puddles are mirrors for silly feet,
Jumping and squishing, oh, what a treat!
Socks soaked through, who would've thought?
That rainy day fun can't be bought.

Nature's fountain, look at it flow,
Each droplet a tickle, a soft little glow.
With squeaky shoes, we go forth and play,
Under the sky, life's splashes display.

So let's embrace what the clouds send down,
In the giggles and grumbles, we won't wear a frown.
With raindrops cheering, our spirits won't rest,
Beneath the cloud's caress, we're all truly blessed.

Liquid Life

Liquid life flows in every stream,
Where fish wear hats and the frogs laugh and dream.
With a splash and a leap, the joy takes flight,
As the sun sets, everything feels just right.

Bubbles rise up from the pools of glee,
As the turtles gossip, 'Hey, look at me!'
A rainbow appears, oh what a surprise,
When waterworks happen, and laughter just flies.

Dance on the shore, let the splashes commence,
Chasing each droplet, it makes perfect sense.
In the dance of the waves, we twirl and sway,
Liquid life bubbles, come join in the play.

So grab a froggie or find you a duck,
Let's splash through the day, who needs a truck?
In the fun of the flow, we find pure delight,
Liquid life's laughter makes everything bright.

Roots of Revival

In the garden, a party is set,
The roots are jiving, they won't forget.
With worms in tuxedos, all dressed so fine,
They wiggle and squirm, saying, 'This is divine!'

Flowers all giggle, their colors they boast,
As the bees come buzzing, creating a toast.
"Cheers to the rain!" the daisies all sing,
While the sun shines bright, it's a glorious thing.

A carrot in the corner, giving a wink,
"Let's dig in the dirt till we can't even think!"
With laughter abounding, roots twist and twirl,
Reviving old memories in their earthy swirl.

So come to the garden, let's make some noise,
With roots of revival, we'll play with joys.
When each drop falls down, it's a giggling spree,
In this playful soil, we're so wild and free.

Graceful Showers

Graceful showers sprinkle with flair,
Dressing the world in a cool, crisp air.
With each little drip, a new dance begins,
As the earth shakes off its old winter sins.

The flowers put on their sparkly caps,
While squirrels wear raincoats, dodging the laps.
A puddle parade lines the muddy lane,
Where ducks quack along in a jovial chain.

Breezes whisper secrets to daisies and ferns,
While raindrops are counting their curvy turns.
In the giggle of droplets, we find the fun,
Graceful showers shine like a sparkle in the sun.

So grab your galoshes and splash on the ground,
In this shower of laughter, let each smile abound.
From the sky to our toes, we're joyfully sown,
In the playful rain, we're never alone.

The Pulse of the Earth

In the garden, socks are wet,
Plants are dancing, no regret.
With the hose like a wild snake,
Who knew flowers could awake?

Sprinklers spin like playful toys,
Chasing down the giggling boys.
Soil is squishy, mud is King,
Watch out now, here comes the fling!

Gnomes are shaking, having fun,
A beetle joins, now it's a run.
Who knew earth could be so spry?
With a splash, the plants all fly!

Nature's party, all around,
Laughter echoes, joyous sound.
Here's to greenery, oh so wild,
Even dirt can act like a child!

Cradled by Clouds

Up in the garden, birds complain,
As I drench the plants, it's plain.
Chasing droplets, oh what fun,
Who knew veggies could all run?

Clouds are laughing, making mist,
While I wave my hose, persist.
Tomatoes blush, they squeal in fright,
"Don't drown us!" they call in the night!

Sunflowers giggle, stretching tall,
Lettuce rolls, oh what a brawl!
"I'm wet, I'm wild!" cries out a sprout,
Making sure it's a fun-filled rout!

In this jungle, chaos reigns,
With watering cans like old trains.
Yet beneath the laughter and play,
The plants grow up, what can I say?

Harvesting the Horizon

On the porch, I fill my cup,
While the garden says, "Fill us up!"
Beans start to whisper, "Let it rain!"
Potatoes giggle, dancing in the grain.

Pumpkins plot a bouncing spree,
"Oh dear friend, won't you let me be?"
With each splash, they cheer and sway,
Offering a joy, come what may!

Radishes boast, "We're the best!"
While zucchinis opt for a jest.
Out in the sun, they all unite,
Together basking in afternoon light!

Harvest time is on the rise,
With laughter blooming in the skies.
Oh what fun to watch them grow,
In this garden of giggles, watch them glow!

Fluid Fantasies

A hose in hand, I feel the flow,
Plants like rockets, ready to go.
Spray a little, hear them sing,
"Make it rain!" the daisies swing!

Buckets flip, oh what a sight,
As I hop and dance, what pure delight!
With a whirl and twirl, I'm a sight to see,
Getting soaked with nature's glee!

Rabbits leap in muddy joy,
Chasing water, oh what ploy!
Each droplet feels like fairy dust,
In the garden, it's a must!

Rainbows twist, as clouds take flight,
Bathtime fun, what a delight!
Nature whispers, "Join the spree,"
In fluid dreams, we laugh with glee!

Kaleidoscope of Cascades

Under the drippy spout, the plants sing,
Chasing each droplet, oh what a fling!
A slipper slips by, just caught in the show,
With every slip-up, laughter will flow.

The garden hose dances, a snake with a wig,
Sending the neighbors into a big gig.
Spraying the cats, who leap with a shout,
This wild, squishy party, who knew it would sprout?

Flowers in tutus, roses on parade,
With every squirt, another grand charade.
Sunflowers spin, their heads in the breeze,
How to stay still when the whole world's a tease?

So here we gather with joy in our hearts,
As droplets become our masterful arts.
Liquid confetti, the blooms' favorite game,
In this colorful cascade, we're all just the same!

Nature's Nourishment

A can in my hands, oh what a delight,
Plants now expect me, a regular sight.
But I'm just a gardener, spilled milkshake spewer,
Making a splash, like a clumsy old skier!

The daisies all giggle, oh what a tease,
As I trample their friends, forget them with ease.
The lilies are snickering, all in good cheer,
Who knew I could make such an uproarious beer?

Throw in a worm, just to spice it a bit,
They wiggle and jiggle, never do quit.
A carefree farmer, chaotic and spry,
As I grunt and I splash, the neighbors all sigh.

Yet somehow, they flourish, my mishaps the key,
With laughter and joy, down comes the free spree.
So fill up your cups, let the chaos unfold,
For natures' own magic in mischief is sold!

Growth in the Gloom

In a foggy old patch, my seedlings reside,
To see them get taller, they need to decide.
I hold my sprayer, a wizard of green,
Spritzing the shadows—what a silly scene!

Lilies in slippers, they dance with a twirl,
While tiny tomatoes go wild for a whirl.
The clouds look on, like a grumpy old man,
While I serenade seedlings, the germination plan.

With beets blushing red, and peas in a flurry,
The garden takes shape, in delightful hurry.
But then here comes thunder, oh what a sight,
They giggle at raindrops like fireworks bright!

So here in the gloom, we find joy in the mess,
With each silly spat, I must confess.
The plants all agree; they've joined the sweet jest,
In our wacky green world, we laugh with the best!

Thirst for Tomorrow

Little critters peek as the sun starts to rise,
They gather suspiciously, those crafty ol' guys.
I whip out my bucket, they scatter and flee,
Too close to the spout, it's a splash-a-thon spree!

My little garden's thirsty, a party in drought,
But every great parade needs a wild little route.
So I dance in the rain, a mud-loving ghost,
And cheers from the daisies, they quip: "What a host!"

With jugs of ambition, I sprinkle the ground,
While the frogs make a band, what a ruckus around!
They leap to the rhythm of giggles and spins,
Even the weeds shout, "Let the fun begin!"

And as day melts away, under twilight's charm,
I water the dreams, keeping everything warm.
For every droplet brings joys to narrate,
These whimsical moments, forever celebrate!

Serene Sojourn

On this day, I water my plants,
They sway and dance like they're in a trance.
My cactus glows, quite the delight,
But still won't hug me, even with all its might.

I trip and spill, oh what a sight,
Soil flies around me, a comical fight.
The ferns are snickering, like they've seen it all,
But my rescue plan? Just laugh and call!

The tulips shout, 'Hey, pour us more!'
I give them a splash; they start to roar.
Sunflowers grin, as if on cue,
Their laughter's contagious, I'm laughing too.

As this chaotic gala comes to an end,
I think to myself, 'Water is a friend.'
Next Wednesday? More juggling, I assume,
I'll be the star of my own plant-filled room!

Elixirs of Life

Gather 'round, my leafy brigade,
Today's the day we mostly parade.
A splash, a dash, all in jest,
Quenching your thirst is our noble quest!

The pot plants whisper, 'Hey, don't be cheap!'
They wiggle their leaves, they're hard to keep.
I chuckle and say, 'It's all in the fun!'
But they just glower, like I'm the one!

A sprinkle of life, a squirt of cheer,
I'm the clumsy gardener; the coast is clear!
Even the weeds have taken their seats,
Expecting a show with their leafy beats.

As I drown my regrets in a can of green,
The roses blush, it's quite the scene!
They tease and they laugh, with petals so bright,
'Elixirs of life? Let's drink them tonight!'

Fluid Flora

In the garden, we play this game,
Plants with faces, all looking the same.
I wield my watering can with flair,
But somehow manage to drench my hair!

The daisies giggle, they think it's grand,
While the poor geraniums can't understand.
"Do we float?" asks one, "Are we turning to fish?"
I say, "Calm down, that's not our dish!"

A sudden glitch, I trip on a weed,
My shoes become a muddy steed.
"Who needs shoes?" I laugh in bliss,
Only this garden could bring such a twist!

With a flourish and twist, I make a grand stand,
That sprightly little fern waves its hand.
"May we invite more chaos, oh please!"
They reach out their roots, eager to tease!

Tranquil Tides

A gentle splash, my garden scheme,
As plants align like a funny dream.
The hydrangeas cheer, colors a-popping,
While I'm busy sneezing, the pollen's just hopping.

The lily pads wink, with a sly little smirk,
They say, "Boy, this guy really is a jerk!"
But with a swift toss of the watering can,
I declare a dance-off, oh yes, I can!

The sunbeams tickle the boughs – they sway,
What a wild show on this sunny display!
I flip like a fish, they giggle and glee,
"Who knew our gardener could dance like a bee?"

With each little drop, humor flows high,
While I'm losing my grip, oh my, oh my!
But laughter does bloom and that's the best part—
Every plant's a friend, with a leafy heart!

Greenery's Grasp

In the garden, I try my best,
To keep those weeds away from the rest.
But every time I bend to pluck,
I trip on roots and bad luck!

The flowers giggle, petals a-flap,
While I'm tangled in a muddy trap.
Their laughter echoes through the trees,
As I dance around, a clumsy breeze.

I water plants with zeal and pride,
But somehow end up soaked outside.
The hose has a mind, it squirts with glee,
Leaving me drenched and laughing with tea!

At least the veggies think it's grand,
As I splash about with garden hand.
For every mishap, there's joy to find,
Greenery's grasp, oh, so unrefined!

The Voice of the River

The river babbles tales of woe,
While I toss in pebbles, 'watch it go!'
It splashes back with a cheery sound,
Teaching me how to dance around.

"Hey there fish, do you hear me splash?"
They dart away in a shiny flash.
The river laughs, "You're all wet too!
But your silly shoes are quite the view!"

A canoe floats by, with folks who shout,
"I'm trying to fish, not have a rout!"
I wave and wiggle, giving them fright,
The river chuckles, "What a sight!"

With every ripple and every wave,
The voice of the river is fun and brave.
So, I skip stones with giddy delight,
Enjoying the chaos from day into night!

Flourishing in the Fog

Fog rolls in, it's a silly scene,
I can't see my plants, nor what they mean.
Did I water them, or forget my task?
I peer and stumble—oh, what a mask!

The flowers call, "We're fine, don't fret!"
While I juggle pots, like a living pet.
A leafy friend whispers jokes in the mist,
And we giggle together, none can resist.

The sun peeks out, a bright, cheeky grin,
I drop the watering can, let the fun begin!
As dew drips down like nature's tears,
Our chuckles meet the morning cheers.

So here we bloom, in our goofy guise,
Flourishing in fog, with misty surprise.
In this garden of humor, we thrive and play,
Growing laughter in a colorful spray!

Raindrops as Reminders

Raindrops dribble, oh, what a game,
On my umbrella, they tap my name.
"Did you water that flower?" they tease with glee,
I nod and smile, oh, look at me!

Each drop's a reminder of garden woes,
As I dodge puddles that put on shows.
The clouds chuckle, "Oh, look at them dance!"
While I splash through mud in a silly prance.

I rush to my plants, all sunny and bright,
But they're already giggling in sheer delight.
"Hey, we're fine! We're wet, it's true,"
They sip from raindrops, a nourishing brew.

So, let it rain, let it pour, let it pour,
With every droplet, I'm never a bore.
For gardens grow best when laughter is loud,
Raindrops as reminders, I dance, feeling proud!

Celestial Waters

In the sky, a hose does fling,
Clouds dance like it's a silly fling.
Rain drops down, a playful splatter,
Umbrellas open, hearts grow fatter.

The puddles laugh with little leaps,
As kids splash through, ignoring heaps.
A dog dashes, joins the fun,
Chasing droplets, he's the one!

Fish swim in their tiny pools,
Waving fins like playful fools.
They gossip 'bout the skies so wet,
"Who knew up there, it'd be a bet?"

So let it pour, let it rave,
We'll dance like dolphins, oh so brave!
With water guns, we start a fight,
On this day, we'll laugh with delight.

Calm in the Current

A duck floats by in perfect style,
While children giggle, just a mile.
The river waves with joyful glee,
"Join me, friends, it's fun to be!"

A fish pops up with a cheeky grin,
"Swim with me, let's make a din!"
But the kids just splash around,
As laughter echoes, joy abounds.

A turtle moves at a steady pace,
In his slow dance, he owns the space.
"C'mon now, let's take it slow,"
"Life's about the fun we sow!"

So let the current take us far,
Where giggles flow and wild hearts spar.
Every splash, a memory made,
In this calm, we feel the shade.

Embracing the Element

With buckets held high, we start the game,
Soaked from the rain, but that's our fame.
Splashes galore, like joy on the street,
We slip and slide, what a funny feat!

A sponge falls down, oh what a mess,
Squeezed by a friend, it causes stress!
New water fights emerge, all in cheer,
"Dodge this splash, or you'll shed a tear!"

A cartoon cloud floats overhead,
Dropping drizzle, as it fled.
"Don't mind me," it seems to say,
"I'm just here to brighten your day."

So raise your cups to the fun in the sun,
Let's chase the waves, forever run.
Laughing together, we make quite the crew,
Embracing the splash with skies so blue!

Breathing in the Blue

A splash of color, a sea of hue,
The playful waves say, 'Come on through!'
With every dip, we giggle out loud,
Come join the fun, let's be water proud.

The piers and boats join the parade,
As laughter and joy begin to cascade.
Fish make faces, they wiggle and dance,
In this splash zone, there's always a chance.

A whale pops up, and winks an eye,
"Dive on in, let's reach the sky!"
"We'll surf on bubbles, dance on the crest,
Together we'll put our skills to the test!"

So breathe in the blue, let your cares drift,
With every bubble, the world feels a lift.
Celebrating life with splashes and cheer,
In a watery world, we shed every fear.

Horizon of Hope

The garden's thirsty, what a sight,
A hose in hand, my fears take flight.
I dance around like a crazy fool,
The plants just watch, they've got the drool.

A splash goes here, a spray goes there,
I get soaked too, but who would care?
The neighbor laughs, I hear him giggle,
While I right my aim and do a little wiggle.

With every drop, my joy does grow,
Some flowers shout, 'Hey, look at our show!'
I'm the maestro of this charming flood,
Just call me the Watering Bud.

With hoses tangled like spaghetti mess,
I proclaim, 'This chaos is my best!'
The sun and I both share a grin,
As I tune my garden to a silly din.

Crystal Clear Dreams

As I fill the bucket, dreams take flight,
Of dancing daisies in the sunlight.
But oops, I trip, what a silly show,
Spraying water like a fountain, oh no!

I watch the ants parade and strut,
While I'm over here, stuck in a rut.
They wave their tiny flags in cheer,
While I'm stuck giggling with a face full of beer.

The hose becomes a garden snake,
I wrestle it, oh, what a mistake!
It squirts me good, in my laughing spree,
This watering task is a comedy!

Crystal drops glisten in the breeze,
My plants now worry, 'Please, not the tease!'
Yet I just laugh and take my stand,
The giddiness grows, oh what a grand plan!

The Essence of Existence

I grab my can and step outside,
To bless each bloom and take pride.
But my aim is off, oh dear me!
I water the dog, he's not so free.

He shakes it off, looks less than pleased,
With every droplet, his fur's now seized.
He gives me a glare, can't say it's shy,
I only laugh as he lets out a sigh.

The plants support me, oh what friends,
They cheer me on as my aim descends.
I'm the court jester with a sparkling crown,
In my tiny kingdom, I never frown.

Existence is funny, with mishaps galore,
Like my neighbor's cat who just loves to explore.
So here's to the chaos, and what it brings,
In this garden of laughter, my heart truly sings!

Vital Vistas

With watering can tucked under my arm,
I set out to spread a little charm.
But my first splash hits me right in the face,
Now I'm the wettest comedian in this place!

Nearby, the flowers are cracking jokes,
'You call that water? We're just some folks!'
I laugh and say, 'Hey, hugs are great!'
They nod along, 'You're a bit late!'

A toad hops by, with quite the leap,
His croaks get louder, 'You're in too deep!'
I splash him too, and what a sight,
A tadpole concert, oh what delight!

Vital vistas come in all shapes and forms,
Even when wet, delightfully warms.
So here's to the giggles and puddles all round,
In this vibrant garden, joy knows no bounds!

Serendipity in the Stream

A fish wore a hat, quite absurd and rare,
It thought it was human, with time to spare.
It danced on a log, made everyone laugh,
As ducks quacked in rhythm, applause for the gaffe.

A frog played the fiddle, on a lily pad stage,
Made jokes about flies, with a comical rage.
The river, it chuckled, swirled with delight,
Under sunlit patter, a whimsical sight.

But soon came a splash, and the party was done,
The fish lost its hat, oh, what a run!
The frog lost its tune, went back to a croak,
While the ducks formed a band, just a bunch of yolk!

Yet every now and then, when summer's in bloom,
The stream tells the tale of its funny costume.
With bubbles of laughter, it flows endlessly,
A spot for the silly, where all want to be.

The Caress of Clouds

Fluffy white cushions drift through the skies,
Tickling the sunbeams while hiding the cries.
A raindrop fell gently, right onto my nose,
I giggled, then slipped, and landed in prose.

Clouds started sneezing, what a ruckus they made,
Droplets like confetti began to cascade.
Umbrellas turned boats, the street was a stream,
As people all danced in the water's wild dream.

Sunbeams and shadows played peek-a-boo games,
Rain jackets became capes with heroic claims.
Who said rainy days would spark little cheer?
We twirled through the puddles, with laughter to hear!

When clouds let it rain, and skies turned to grey,
I laughed with the breezes that blew me away.
So here's to the droplets and each silly splash,
For a day filled with fun is a day that won't crash!

Fragile Ferns

Once grew a fern that fancied a wig,
It donned layers of leaves, feeling quite big.
Neighbors all chuckled, 'How fancy can a plant be?'
But the fern just smiled, claiming, 'Look at me!'

With roots set in soil, it danced with the breeze,
Flaunting its fronds with incredible ease.
A squirrel ran by, calling, 'Oh, look at that!'
'What a peculiar, leafy-haired aristocrat!'

But when raindrops came, oh, how it did shiver,
Its wig turned to mush, oh what a river!
It sighed with relief when the sun greeted back,
And started a fashion week, planning its next act.

Now every week, it struts in the light,
With a crown of fine dewdrops, glittering bright.
So here's to the ferns with dreams made of cheer,
May they never lose their sense of sheer weird!

The Fountain of Life

In the town square stood a fountain so grand,
With splashes that danced like a mysterious band.
People tossed coins, wishes whispered with glee,
While pigeons just laughed, living carefree.

One day it erupted, a stream of surprise,
Spraying all onlookers, oh, what a prize!
Kiddos with bubbles jumped high in delight,
While grown-ups all shrieked, what a hilarious sight!

They wrung out their shirts, sharing laughter and fun,
The fountain a jester, who'd only begun.
With a spray and a splash, it tickled the street,
A joy-filled eruption, no one could compete!

So every now and then, when the sun's shining bright,
The fountain laughs back, a whimsical sight.
And amidst all the droplets, joy wakes the wise,
In the dance of the splashes, pure laughter lies.

The Heartbeat of Hydration

In a garden so lush, I dance with glee,
A hose in my hand, oh, look at me!
I'll drown all the weeds, they won't stand a chance,
While squirrels and bunnies join in my prance.

With droplets of joy, I giggle and spray,
The petals are laughing, they shine like the day.
But watch out, dear friend, the puddles are sly,
One slip in the mud, I'm a gurgling guy!

The flowers are thirsty, they beg for a sip,
Each splash reveals a new plant's quick quip.
A daffodil chuckles, "Hey, buddy, I'm dry!"
While daisies chime in, "Oh, can't let that fly!"

So here I stand, in a water-filled trance,
With laughter and plants, oh, come join the dance.
For hydration's a blast, we're all in this game,
To blossom and grow, and never feel lame.

Vale of Verdancy

In a vale of excitement, where laughter takes form,
A drizzle gives life, oh it's never a bore!
Each plant's got a secret, they giggle and sway,
As I wield my canteen like it's a grand ballet.

The daisies yell, "More! We need a good drink!"
While marigolds whisper, "Come on, don't overthink!"
I'm the water magician, they cheer and they shout,
With each little splash, there's no room for doubt.

Little droplets leap like they're playing tag,
While roots hold their breath, not a single brag.
"Who's the champion then?" asks a sprightly fern,
"Let's make this a contest; it's my turn to learn!"

A battle of blooms, who'll grow up the best?
So spritz with a chuckle, let's put them to test.
In this vale of verdancy, let laughter abound,
For joy in this garden is where love is found.

Seeds of Silence

On a quiet Wednesday, I stroll with my can,
The peas are all giggling, oh what a plan!
With a splash and a dash, I feel quite the ace,
But tomatoes are shushing, "We need some space!"

The beans are all whispering, plotting their rise,
While carrots complain, "Oh, we've got our spies!"
I'll quench their thirst while respecting their vow,
But calling it "silent" seems hard to allow!

As I sprinkle their roots with a lighthearted cheer,
A squash pipes up, "Whoa, I'm starting to fear!"
"Did he just call us quiet? We're louder than that!"
While lettuce adds softly, "Show off your hat!"

I giggle and chuckle, in this merry plight,
For every green sprout seems to know how to fight.
With laughter and love, let's give it a whirl,
Seeds of silence, now let's give that a twirl!

Weaving with Water

With garden shears ready, I start my grand day,
Weaving with water, oh what a ballet!
The potted plants cheer as I thread them with streams,
A tapestry shining of nature's bright dreams.

The tulips are swooning as I sprinkle their tips,
While petunias crack jokes with whimsical quips.
"Just look at our sprinkle! It's like a soft trance!"
"Hold on to your roots; it's a persnickety dance!"

The herbs in the corner are cooking up plans,
They whisper of flavors in simmering pans.
"Let's host a feast once the sun's fully set,
With flavors and laughter, our party's the bet!"

So here in this garden, we twirl and we spin,
With each little drop, let the fun times begin.
Weaving with water, oh what a delight,
In the heart of the garden, we frolic till night!

www.ingramcontent.com/pod-product-compliance
Lightning Source LLC
Chambersburg PA
CBHW072117070526
44585CB00016B/1483